T0094462

THINGS AS IT IS

BOOKS BY CHASE TWICHELL

Things as It Is

*Horses Where the Answers Should Have Been: New
    and Selected Poems*

Dog Language

The Lover of God (translations of Rabindranath
    Tagore, with Tony K. Stewart)

The Snow Watcher

The Ghost of Eden

*The Practice of Poetry: Writing Exercises from
    Poets Who Teach* (co-edited with Robin Behn)

Perdido

The Odds

Northern Spy

CHASE TWICHELL

Things as It Is

COPPER CANYON PRESS

Port Townsend, Washington

Copyright 2018 by Chase Twichell

All rights reserved

Printed in the United States of America

Cover art: Bill Traylor, American, 1854–1949; *Untitled* (*Two Dogs Fighting*), ca. 1939–42; poster paint and graphite on cardboard; 16.5 × 21.125 inches; High Museum of Art, Atlanta, T. Marshall Hahn Collection, 1997.116

Copper Canyon Press is in residence at Fort Worden State Park in Port Townsend, Washington, under the auspices of Centrum. Centrum is a gathering place for artists and creative thinkers from around the world, students of all ages and backgrounds, and audiences seeking extraordinary cultural enrichment.

LIBRARY OF CONGRESS CATALOGING-IN-PUBLICATION DATA

Names: Twichell, Chase, 1950– author.
Title: Things as it is / Chase Twichell.
Description: Port Townsend, Washington : Copper Canyon Press, 2018. |
  Includes bibliographical references.
Identifiers: LCCN 2018018101 | ISBN 9781556595493 (pbk. : alk. paper)
Subjects: LCSH: Life—Poetry. | Change—Poetry.
Classification: LCC PS3570.W47 A6 2018 | DDC 811/.54—dc23
LC record available at https://lccn.loc.gov/2018018101

9 8 7 6 5 4 3 2 FIRST PRINTING

Copper Canyon Press
Post Office Box 271
Port Townsend, Washington 98368

www.coppercanyonpress.org

ACKNOWLEDGMENTS

Gratitude to the editors of the following publications, in which poems first appeared, some in earlier forms:

Academy of American Poets Poem-a-Day: "Downstairs in Dreams," "Never," "The Phantoms for Which Clothes Are Designed"

The American Journal of Poetry: "Ghost Dress," "A Pond in Japan"

The American Poetry Review: "The Feeder of Strays," "Keene Valley Elegy," "Plain American," "The Second Arrow," "Tiny White Spirals"

The Cortland Review: "The Portors"

The Cumberland River Review: "The Missing *Weekly Reader*s," "Soft Leather Reins"

The Dark Horse (UK): "Before the Ash," "Bermuda Sand," "The Floatisphere," "What the Trees Said"

Domestic Cherry (UK): "Bermuda Sand," "Falling Leaves," "Sickness and Medicine," "Silence vs. Music"

Field: "Before the Ash"

Fifth Wednesday Journal: "Days of Not-Knowing"

The Georgia Review: "What's Wrong with Me"

H.O.W. Journal: "Early Snow," "Sickness and Medicine"

I-70 Review: "Bermuda Sand," "Dark Slides," "The Floatisphere," "Herds of Humans," "A Strange Little Animal"

The Massachusetts Review: "A River in Egypt," "What the Trees Said"

The Moth (UK): "Spaciousness"

Narrative: "Birdsong," "Ermine Tails," "The Hill Towns of Connecticut," "Mom Looking Skinny," "The New Dark Ages," "Now's Dream"

New England Review: "Ancient Questions," "Spaciousness"

The New Yorker: "Roadkill"

Northwest Review: "Falling Leaves," "Silence vs. Music"

Passages North: "Crickets at the End of the World," "Mom's Playthings," "Strangers' Houses"

Plume: "Animals, Not Initials," "Burning Leaves," "The Children's Prison," "Fireworks or Gunfire?," "Handwriting's Ancestors," "I Keep Scaring Myself," "Maverick," "Mom's Party," "Mom's Red Convertible," "No Blue Allowed," "Nothing" (as "Practice"), "Snapshot with Eyes Turned Away," "Two Dogs Passing Through the Yard," "You, Reader, as I Imagine You"

The Plume Anthology of Poetry 6: "Labradorite," "Winter Crows"

Poet Lore: "Nan's Stick," "Radio Silence"

Poetry: "The Ghost of Tom," "The Lullabies of Elsewhere"

Provincetown Arts: "Buzzyboy"

The Rialto (UK): "Babylon at Stonehenge," "Booby-Trapped Weapons," "Roadkill"

Salmagundi: "Babylon at Stonehenge," "Booby-Trapped Weapons," "Cages for Unknown Animals," "The Cloisters," "Earth Without Humans," "Fast Stars," "Graveyard of Imaginary Selves," "Kenshō of Ash," "Private Ceremony," "Sad Song," "Spiral," "Toygers"

Saranac Review: "In One Ear," "Zazen"

The Southampton Review: "Things as It Is," "The Wrong House"

Tricycle: "After Snow," "Fox Bones," "Invisible Fence"

Women's Studies: "The Background," "The Duck Boat," "Movies of Mountains," "A Red-Hot X," "The Uphill River"

The Yale Review: "Cloud Seeding," "Early Winter Wilderness," "The Ends of the World," "Her Ashes," "Murder and Mayhem in Miami," "My Bob Dylan," "The Words of His Dementia"

‡

"Bermuda Sand" was published in a limited edition by Pressed Wafer as part of the One Fund Boston, a project to help victims of the Boston Marathon bombings.

"The M Sound" was published as a broadside at Hamilton College.

For my Odysseus, Russell Banks

One day while editing a transcription of Suzuki Rōshi's first lecture on the *Sandōkai,* I came upon the phrase "things as it is." I asked him if perhaps he had not meant to say "things as they are," which I thought to be proper syntax.

"No," he said, "what I meant is 'things as it is.'"

DAVID CHADWICK

Contents

The Ghost of Tom

Strangers' Houses   5

The Missing *Weekly Reader*s   6

Maverick   8

Spiral   9

Snapshot with Eyes Turned Away   10

A Red-Hot X   11

The Children's Prison   12

Burning Leaves   13

The Hill Towns of Connecticut   14

Downstairs in Dreams   16

The Cloisters   17

The Ghost of Tom   18

Soft Leather Reins   20

Lederhosen   21

Radio Silence   23

Dark Slides   24

Private Ceremony   26

First Boyfriend   27

My Bob Dylan   28

Early Winter Wilderness   29

Sad Song   30

Graveyard of Imaginary Selves   32

Earth Without Humans

Before the Ash   37

Cloud Seeding   38

The Ends of the World   40

Booby-Trapped Weapons   43

The Background   44

After Snow   45

Crickets at the End of the World   46

A Strange Little Animal   47

Earth Without Humans   49

The New Dark Ages   50

Tiny White Spirals   51

Herds of Humans   53

Birdsong   54

Keene Valley Elegy   55

What the Trees Said   57

Always Elsewhere

A Pond in Japan   61

Mom's Party   62

The Portors   63

In One Ear   65

The Uphill River   66

Mom's Playthings   67

The Lullabies of Elsewhere   68

No Blue Allowed   69

Bermuda Sand   70

Mom Looking Skinny   71

Mom's Red Convertible   73

Babylon at Stonehenge   74

The Floatisphere   77

Movies of Mountains   78

Handwriting's Ancestors   79

The Words of His Dementia   80

Ermine Tails   81

Animals, Not Initials   83

The M Sound   84

Her Ashes   85

Roadkill

You, Reader, as I Imagine You 89

Cages for Unknown Animals 90

Nothing 91

Roadkill 92

Invisible Fence 93

Spaciousness 94

Zazen 95

Never 96

The Second Arrow 97

Silence vs. Music 99

Labradorite 100

Sickness and Medicine 101

Path of Red Leaves 102

Early Snow 103

Days of Not-Knowing 104

I Keep Scaring Myself 105

Falling Leaves 106

Nan's Stick 107

Fox Bones 108

Two Dogs Passing Through the Yard 109

Now's Dream

The Park from Above 113

The Feeder of Strays 114

Bipolar II-ity 115

The Duck Boat 116

Buzzyboy 118

A River in Egypt 120

Ghost Dress 121

The Phantoms for Which Clothes Are Designed 122

Murder and Mayhem in Miami 123

The Wrong House   125
Fireworks or Gunfire?   126
Ancient Questions   128
Now's Dream   129
What's Wrong with Me   130
Toygers   131
Plain American   132
Things as It Is   134
Kenshō of Ash   135
Winter Crows   137
Fast Stars   138

Notes   141
About the Author   143

THINGS AS IT IS

The Ghost of Tom

Strangers' Houses

The greenhouse door
was kept locked, but kids
knew about the key.

Inside were aisles of orchids.
It was like being inside a cloud.

Can that be real?

That I played in strangers' houses
when they were out,
and no one ever knew?

The same people had a water
garden, with a lion-face fountain
and small gold koi with lace tails.

Can they live under the ice?

No, Stupid, said a boy.
They get new ones every spring.

The Missing *Weekly Reader*s

One Sunday noon at 436
(Gram's house—the entire family

referred to their houses
by street number),

the first big snow was falling.

We sat around the table
in an igloo: the dining room

darkened and hushed,
windows a swollen glow.

After lunch, the cousins
split up to play. Sam and I
roamed the neighborhood,

slipping invisible
behind the schoolyard's

white chenille chain link.

We looted the small covered
bridge of the mailbox with great care,
disturbing no snow.

Only Sam and I know where
the *Weekly Reader*s for the week
of February 16, 1958, reside.

If you someday find them
in a surprising place, with a note
from some kids admitting to the theft,

please keep it to yourself.

Maverick

I spent my one allowed hour per week
of television with Dad. *Maverick.*

I'd completely forgotten about the line
Smooth as the handle on a gun,
though I'd sung all the rest by heart

for many years. Still sing, when alone.

Who is the tall, dark stranger there?
Maverick is the name

(though I misremembered it
as Maverick is *his* name).

Dad corrected papers as we watched
(Latin teacher).

We liked the riverboats,
poker games, and six-shooters,
Natchez to New Orleans.

I knew what
living on jacks and queens meant,
and the rank of hands.

I wasn't really a tomboy.
I didn't want to be a boy.

I wanted to not be a girl.

Spiral

At the very center is a seed
in a permanent state of splitting.

Inside it a neighbor lifts
a four-year-old girl onto the mantel,
cold marble, and looks at her.

Then a photographer dresses her
in costumes that reveal
her secret place.

My first love promised
to come back and never did.

My father told my cousin
I would make the world's worst wife.

I saw what the boys did to the dog.

What I call my self was innocent
once, I suppose, an unsplit seed,

but I have no proof.

Snapshot with Eyes Turned Away

Here's a nurse with a vial of candy pills
and a miniature stethoscope, one finger raised
to the camera: *I don't want to be looked.*

Mom still quotes me when she sees me
self-conscious in photographs:
You still don't want to be looked!

The photographer took the nurse
to his basement studio. The cowgirl too.

Also a mermaid with slinky, dragging tail.

Mom was right upstairs, in his house,
when he moved aside the tail to get the shot.

A Red-Hot X

Wallpaper at Grandma's had broncos,
campfires, and cowboys branding calves.

Wherever I looked, two men knelt
over a hog-tied calf, holding a stick

with a red-hot X at the tip.

I imagined the wound, the shock
to the mind. Would the calf forget?

Was there somewhere the calf could hide?

When I groom the dog, I study
his haunch, where a brand would go,

how thin the skin is over the muscle,
how shiveringly responsive.

Whenever I think of it they burn the calf again.

The Children's Prison

Everyone's born in one, a prison.

Some parents keep children in,
some let them out.

Even the ones kept in
get out someday.

The grown-ups change the story's ending.

The man—a neighbor, standing
in the garden with a cut-up potato—

told the child that the eyes
just erupting into pale fingers

would someday reach for her hand.
That turned out to be true.

But no one ever saw any potatoes.

The vines flowered, but by then
the girl was already gone.

Burning Leaves

Leaf fires smell like
saddle soap, manure, fresh hay.

Leaf burning's illegal now,
but I remember fathers

letting kids tend the weak,
feathery fires in the street.

I rode my bike through
the ash piles to school.

On my fast horse
I rode everywhere.

One of the men at the stable
liked little girls,

the little, little ones
astride the pony's knobby spine.

Imagine him
passing freely among us,

feeding us sugar cubes, aroused
by our anuses and not-yet-cunts.

The Hill Towns of Connecticut

Dust motes fell from the rafters
all the way down into hay spiced

with manure, molasses in the feed,

and always a man, a stable hand
or somebody's friend.

Girls and horses in the hill towns
of Connecticut—

such freedom, unimaginable now.

Bareback, still flat-chested,
kid-muscles wedding the beasts',

we rode through open fields
to the hole of shadow at the woods' edge,

a tunnel just greening with leaves
in still-closed infant clusters,

though the red buds of the maples
were already falling.

We tracked woodsmoke
to someone's secret camp.

The wife was bent over the hood.
They had a fire going, down to coals.

The husband met my eyes. He looked sad.
He looked away.

I almost forgot about that.

That, and the man who appeared
in a dust beam

to a daydreaming girl with a currycomb,

and slow-danced her up against the horse,
holding her hand against him

beneath his hand,
saying *How, oh how does it feel?*

Just say out loud how it feels and I'll stop.

Downstairs in Dreams

Trying to fall asleep,

I count down stone steps
into the dark, and there they are:

centaurs, half in and half out
of the woods, hindquarters still trees.

Downstairs in dreams I look
directly into their man-eyes,

which are opaque, absorbent.

They don't speak. I don't speak
of the long yellow teeth tearing off

the little dress—just for a glimpse,
no harm done. No hands, no harm.

Their hindquarters still trees.

No words to explain or contain it.

You can't translate something
that was never in a language
in the first place.

The Cloisters

After the eighth grade gaped
at the monkey-people and other weirdos
clinging to the stone acanthi of the columns,

and shoved one another closer to the mask—
half face, half skull—in a crepuscular hall,

and paused at the gap-toothed lion
drooling into his fishless fountain,

it was time for the bus home.

Lying in the sparse underbrush
near the parking lot was a Kotex.

The boys gathered around it.
One of them stabbed it with a stick,

right on the blood spot.

The Ghost of Tom

At family gatherings,
a Family Friend liked gathering
the girls to make us sing rounds.

We always wanted the spooky one,
Have you seen the ghost of Tom?
Long white bones with the rest all gone…

We'd substitute words, like long white *boners*

with the rest all gone,
which he pretended not to hear

because who knows, any one of us
might blow his cover at any minute,

unpredictable little liars that we are,
the girl cousins, talking preteen trash
about him, the things he likes to do,

for instance, gather the girl cousins
and make us sing against our wills.

His personal favorite was
Tender Shepherd, tender Shepherd,

Let me help you count your sheep.
One in the meadow, two in the garden,

Three in the nursery, fast asleep.

One Christmas there were only
three of us, so we sang

the round with one part missing.
I still listen to the fourth part—

that's the real ghost.

Soft Leather Reins

Soft leather reins, dark brown,
just bridle and bareback,
light rain, radiant woods.

Later the horses tangled
with some barbed wire,
but we freed them.

Sound: inchworms feeding,
their droppings falling.
Shots, but far off.

Sally and I rode through childhood
together. We got home at dusk.
There my knowledge ends.

Lederhosen

I said to my sister,
Let's go to Lake Placid tomorrow.

We could drink iced tea on a balcony
overlooking the Lake Placid of our youth—

1966, sixteen and fourteen,
dropped off and picked up by Mom.

Lake Placid nicknamed itself
Little Switzerland around then,

touting its Alpine summers
and wintertime icy descents.

The clock-shop cuckoos all cuckooed at once.

Gingerbread chalets infected
the architecture of the town.

The Swiss Shop had every size of lederhosen
from infants' to men's XXL,
with embroidered suspenders.

Dad had a pair he wore to cocktail parties.

A few of the boys had hand-me-downs,
the older the better—

horn buttons (or bone),
soft, darkened deerskin
covering their loins,

boys from any century,
descended from fauns,

first love somewhere among them.

We fingered the lederhosen
and twirled the earring displays,

ears not yet pierced by Doc Goff
who used common sense to do the job.

Nurse Polly held the ice cube, then the cork.

Radio Silence

In 1957 the Russians sent Sputnik
trespassing out among the stars,
feebly blinking, announcing

the start of the Permanent War.

The whole family lay on the cold grass
watching, even the dogs.

Space was once a clean and perfect mystery.

God lived there. As a kid I always worried
I was faking it when I prayed, as if both of us

were pretending we could hear the other
through tin cans and a piece of string.

There was silence where the voice
was meant to be.

Sputnik reminds me of Laika,
first dog in space. Her skeleton is still
out there somewhere,

poor Moscow street dog
adrift in the complete unknown.

Laika means "barker."

Dark Slides

A lot of them are underexposed,
sometimes too dark
to see who it is, then suddenly

a garden—was it ours?
Dad's baby carrots—

are they a memory?
Something I yearn for?
Something I invented?

And here's poor Eva,
throwing her head around,

blood-flecked froth at the bit.

I'm fourteen, riding saddle-seat.
Her tail has been broken
and set so as to look spirited.

It looks broken.

Gram is wearing a silly hat
with a big white bird on the brim,

wings spread, as if just landing.

Aunt Harmony's clutching cocktail
and cigarette in one hand.

Maybe fifteen, in my first bikini
and puckered white rubber bathing cap—

I don't feel pretty, so I don't look pretty.

Someone has abandoned a sled
in the snow, its slats just whitening.

Footprints, but no humans visible.
Who saved this one, and why?

Private Ceremony

I took my first vows
at barely fifteen—looking up

into the leaves of a paper birch
and beyond that the blue-gray sky,

never still in the mountains
but living, building and dispersing,

moving both toward and away
from my eyes. I saw the leaves'
fine serrations, the red-brown twigs

just starting to ruckle and pale.

There was nothing at all
between those cells and my own.

At that moment the first thunder
entered the atmosphere, a shiver.

First thunder, then shiver, then vow.

First Boyfriend

I'm back in touch with my first
boyfriend, John. He's a tree doctor
in Laos, and a single parent.

Writing to him is unsettling because
it shakes the girl who was there
from her long-standing sleep.

Above the bed in someone's
guest room, someone had written
fuck you in calligraphy on the ceiling.

Then a long bus ride home alone,
small town to small town.

No two loves the same,
but ever afterward

an absence makes itself known.

My Bob Dylan

Back then, everybody knew the music:
the brash, young, coarsely grated voice,

the words that said *Shut up and listen.*

August in the north country,
that's my Bob Dylan.
You have your own.

The cold brook of first love.
The sound of something passing.

Rain on the tent.
Rain hissing in the fire.

Early Winter Wilderness

Woof woof growl—a chainsaw,

followed by the smell of two-cycle oil,
one of the dark scents: woodsmoke,

Packer's Pine Tar Soap,
black with white suds

in the icy brook. His body.
White suds in the icy black brook.

Smoke and pine tar
are what come back to me now.

Gunfire and hammering.
It's hunting season.

Everyone's trying
to get things framed in
before snow.

Sad Song

It's ridiculous, at my age,
to have to pull the car onto the shoulder

because Bob Dylan and Johnny Cash
are singing "Girl from the North Country,"

taking turns remembering not one girl,
but each of their girls, one and then the other,

a duet that forces tears from my eyes
so that I have to pull off the road and weep.

Ridiculous! My sadness is fifty years old!

It travels into sorrow and gets lost there.

Not because it calls up first love, though it does,
or first loss of love, though both
are shawls it wears to hide its wound,

a wound to the girl of which
all men sing, the girl split open,

the sluice through which all of childhood pours,

carrying her out of one country
into another, in which she grows up
wearing a necklace of stones,

one for each girl not her,

though they all live together here
in the north country, where the winds

hit heavy on the borderline.

Graveyard of Imaginary Selves

Mom told me that at one year old
I stood in my crib and watched

the two of them drive off to a party.
She wondered whether that caused

me any lasting psychological damage.
Here lies that one-year-old,

along with all the little shucked-off
waifs and animals I played,
my eyes their eyes—

dog-horse-deer girl,
fluent in animal languages.

And the little tomboy,
spying from the woods.

No one is that child anymore.

I left her in the beautiful
now-gone, never-there playgrounds.

Love's teenage girlfriend's
still hanging around,

the one with a sadness
she could never name.

Here she lies among the others:
the girl with an apron pocket
full of clothespins, in a long skirt,

hanging the wild-armed shirts
of a man gone away again.

And here's the writer first venturing
into the wilderness of words,

the thrilling permanent loneliness.

On each headstone it says,
Don't try to translate.

*We have a private language
you no longer know.*

Each time I come here, I swear
it will be the last time I leave

half of a small blue eggshell, tiger lilies,
pinecones, or icicles on my graves.

Earth Without Humans

Before the Ash

I know not with what weapons
World War III will be fought,

said Albert Einstein, *but World War IV*
will be fought with sticks and stones.

All the killing, centuries of it.

Where will we bury all the bones?

No need to worry. In the end,
no one will be doing any burying.

Let's go back and live in Pompeii,
where olives burst from the trees
and all the dogs are still alive.

Before the ash,
and with ignorance of the ash.

Cloud Seeding

On the news, a man explained
the science of cloud seeding,

how they could drop dry ice
into the clouds to make them rain.

Imagine it raining only at night,
he said, *and sunny every day!*

His words stabbed at the god in me,

the god of weather still ignorant of us,
the clever despoilers.

I wanted a horse, prayed for a horse,
pledged my troth to a horse.

Please, whoever you are,
let a horse come to me
before I turn eleven.

No horse came.
Eleven came and went.

Alan Shepard hit two golf balls
on the moon and left them there.

Now the sky is full of space junk,
some of which falls to earth,

though the chances of it killing anyone
are slight. The only thing it kills

is a ghost horse grazing
in Eden's gray remains.

The Ends of the World

When planes bound for Europe
take off late at night flying due west,

their sound comes to me
as wind in deep winter, slanting
the snow in the empty woods,

forming bright scars, ridges of drift.

Then I wake in the tropics'
air-conditioned chill.

When some grief overtakes me,
my mind flees north
to the clear-crashing brooks,

sun and shucked-off ice,
seeds splitting in the compost.

It was real. I lived there
when any moving water
was safe to drink.

Look, here come some Jet Skis,
gunning up to the public boat launch.

In this world, the mango sky
silhouettes the glass and steel
aspirations of our kind,

then weakens over the towers,
the derricks and cargo ships.

Just look at the guttering back of the bay,
and all that flees from it—

grand wound festering—what a sunset!

Even the mango's abandoning the sky,
hitching a final ride
on the clouds' undersides.

At first I raged at a single soda bottle
aloft on a see-through wave.

Now I no longer want to see
the illusion of the ocean intact,

the not-blue not-green water
breaking open and closing again,
restless above its heart of garbage,

the frothing white sucking edge

depositing a toothbrush, flip-flop,
bald head of a doll, and the usual
deflated jellyfish of condoms,

shoals of cigarette filters still intact
after who knows how long at sea,

a vast and senseless migration—
inedible, immortal, everywhere.

Part of me wants to see the city
gone entirely dark, glittering tableaux
extinguished, nothing but ruins,

colorless permanent shadows
inhabiting the empty streets.

How hard I fall out of sleep,
out of a vision of the earth restored.

I open my eyes in the dark, and find myself
back in the Garden of Earthly Delights,
naked again among stingers and fangs,

extinct and future creatures, all of us
unnamed and equal under the only sky.

But art can't resurrect it.
It only dreams it.

It hands a drunk an empty bottle.

Booby-Trapped Weapons

Governments labor to keep their doctored-weapons programs
secret, in part because they are potentially indiscriminate and
often provide enemy forces with working ammunition, with
which the rigged ammunition has been mixed. The tactic can
also jeopardize friendly forces, causing casualties or destroying
weapons among government troops or proxies—raising political
sensitivities and eroding morale.

C.J. Chivers in the *New York Times,* October 20, 2012

I've tried a hundred times to break
into these two sentences,

to find loose rivets or a bad weld,
but they're beautifully made
and wear no camouflage.

They're like math, which I've never
been able to do in my head.

I understand the words,
but they form a cloud.

The Background

Snow hushes the secret rooms of the woods,

where in summer ferns in the undergloom
unfurl their slow green feathers.

The sky glitters with garbage and cargo.

I read the *Evening News of the War,*
about the death of everything.

That's all there is—the sound of snow

in the inner ear, sound with nowhere
else to go. The background.

After Snow

I'm the first car after the sander.
The cinnamon swirls of fresh sand are intact.

Except for that—the sand and the road—

the woods look as they might have
a thousand years ago, except for

the absence of tracks.

Crickets at the End of the World

Right now it's crossover time,
grasshoppers still razzing the field
as the crickets tune up.

It always surprises me when someone
confuses grasshoppers and crickets.

They say the same words:
Don't love us, we're going away,

but crickets are smaller, more like bullets,
harder to see, night insects,
dark in the dark grass.

The cricket's voice is more strident
than that of the grasshopper—

the words are the same,
but their song knows it's about to end.

A Strange Little Animal

It's a strange little thing—
never seen one before.

Scaly, like a lizard on the warm slate,

but violet, with glassy green quills
and a ridge of soft blond hair down its back

to the tips of its two tails.

All around us the field's lit with fire colors,
yarrow and daisies and hawkweed,

the wind delving into it here and there,
stirring up the coals in the last light.

The strange little animal's lips are moving,
and its eyes look directly into mine,

expressive of something like sadness.

I lean down to hear the words
its mouth seems to be forming,

careful in case it attacks me,
in case it's venomous.

Framing the guttering landscape
in the parenthesis of its tails,

and in a tone I can only describe as apologetic,
it says, *All this is ours now.*

Earth Without Humans

A guy on the street asked me if I could
imagine Earth with no human beings.

I replied that for twenty years I've been
unable to imagine anything else.

Having imagined it, where am I now?
Do I have clear coordinates?

Could a satellite find me?
A dog could find me.

The New Dark Ages

Thunderstorms stir me up—
the stillness right before

the first close tremor,
the pond shivering

at the height of summer,
the field full-blown, going to seed.

But this storm scares me.
A foreign climate occupies the land.

When nature was God, in my childhood,
I wasn't afraid. Snow buried the town,

the river flooded it,
lightning set the woods on fire.

In months the damage bandaged itself
with mosses and ferns.

This storm comes from another
world, here by mistake,

its rain blistering the birch leaves.
Has it been weaponized?

No one knows what to expect
of a storm with human parents.

Tiny White Spirals

Census, August 1, 2016

Number of insects never before
seen in this valley: 5.

1. 1.25". Wingless.
   Gray-and-white reptilian
   pattern on back. No apparent head.

2. Looks like a dung beetle but twice the size.
   Pincers at both ends.

3. 2". Aquatic insect or crustacean?
   Black carapace, corporate logo
   embossed in silver on underside.

4. A hatch of tiny white spirals
   in the pond. No idea.

The dog has made friends
with one of the weirdest:

5. Scarab-like but square, 5",
   color of cherries. It hums and clicks,

and Rebus responds by dipping his head,
which he does when he thinks
something is funny.

Almost every day the two of them
sit together on the big rock by the pond.

I know it's the same one because
it's missing one of its long horns.

A dog and a bug. Anything can happen now.

Herds of Humans

Look in the eye of the dolphin,
the eye of the rat. The animals know
what we decline to know.

Herds of displaced humans
arm themselves against as many
kinds of death as they can imagine.

Cloud death.
Death of the trees.
Death of all the laws.

The four winds wince when they pass
too close to a blade, too close
to a fragment of bone or glass.

Here comes a feral dog, drawn by
the fat in the fire, a little taste of it,
a lick of it, a scrap, a bone.

Birdsong

We strained all the fish from the waters
of the world, both fresh and salt, and ate them.

Pried the last of the secretive, pallid squid

from their crevices and ate them,
sucked snails from their shells.

Next the birds, because birdsong
won't keep other animals alive.

Mammals stopped breeding. We ate them all.
Reptiles lay starving in the sun until we

scaled them and ate their cold-blooded meat.

Most amphibians vanished on their own.
Drifts of feathers buried the shells and bones.

Now the insects outnumber us
two hundred million to one.

The worms, billions to one.

Earth without animals comes before
Earth without humans. We starve last.

The trees are dropping sickened leaves,

too few to cover us when we lie down
at life's end, after the insects and worms.

Keene Valley Elegy

A big storm like this used to
thrill me, a visit from a god,

thirty-six inches and still snowing!

But now I know about the great
floating continents of plastic

twice the size of Texas,
in the Atlantic and Pacific both,

and their spawn the microbeads,

so although the laden woods look
much as they did when I was born,

snow is a mock consecration to me now.

Still, it's a thrill to see the human world
struck dumb and whited out,

an ocean of motionless waves,

no cars, no lights, no music,
only the illusion of Earth

as it was before I understood
it was I who had made it a god.

In summer Russell and I
hunt for chanterelles, which the snails
will devour if they find them first,

and scavenge a few high ledges
for inky wild blueberries,

scant handfuls. First love, last love.
I'm glad my last love is not for a god.

I refuse to wake up again in a graveyard
with neither flowers nor words for the dead.

What the Trees Said

The trees have begun to undress.
Soon snow will come to bandage
the whole wounded world.

When I was young I eloped
with the sky. I wore blue-black,
with underlit ribbons of pink.

I asked the trees
if they would be our witness,
but the trees said no.

Always Elsewhere

A Pond in Japan

I told Mom about a pond I saw in Japan,
how due to the small sculpted hills
and undulating shore, rocks and dwarf pines,

nowhere on its circumference was there
a vantage from which one could see
the pond in its entirety.

That's not possible, said Mom.

Mom's Party

Maria arranged dahlias in a vase
Mom thought was too tall for them.

The caterers passed tenderloin
with horseradish on toast, miniature crab cakes,
and asparagus wrapped in prosciutto.

Yellow caution tape outlined the doors
to the deck. No one fell. The ocean rose and fell.

The ladies said, *Isn't it just like Ann
to know about a band like this?
I must get their name.*

She was glimpsed among dahlias
and lilies, both presence and absence.

Most of the guests were octogenarians.
They arrived promptly at 5:30
and did not overstay.

No one left without having had
a word with Ann, silver mermaid

shawled in the last gleaming
sea of her element,
both presence and absence.

The Portors

Whenever Mom's on the phone,
she can hear the Portors
talking in the background.

The Por*ters*? *No, it's Por*tors, *with two o's.*
That's how they spell it.
*Bill and What's-her-name Por*tor.

Who are they? What do they talk about?

How the hell should she know?
She doesn't eavesdrop. They natter
in the wires, the wind, the airwaves.

And that's all there is to say about the Por*tors.*

She drinks white wine, I drink red.
We're laughing about all kinds
of crazy things from the past,

like the time Dad took her duck hunting
and the two of them lay invisible in poison ivy,
newly engaged, off to a bad start.

When her memory goes wandering,
she follows it, the two of them

headed for wherever it is I'm also bound
after the stories and the wine,

the other funerals and the giving away
of all but the very favorite things,
just enough to furnish one room.

I'm not worried, not afraid.
I'll have Bill and What's-her-name for company.

In One Ear

Even as a young man Uncle Dave
scrambled all his maxims,

so when his dementia began to move
the furniture without asking,

and all of us became someone else's relatives
there by mistake and talking about things
he'd never heard of, Dave said,

Well, in one ear and gone tomorrow,

which we all agreed was profound,
though no one could say why.

The Uphill River

When Mom asked me about Zen,
I said, Everything changes. All we can do
is stop trying to swim upstream.

We were unpacking dishes
in her new apartment, Unit 2310,

with windows overlooking lawns,
then fields, then the flowering banks

of the Uphill River, with gently graded
paths for strolling, sturdy handrails,
and many benches along the way.

I said, Remember Gram
telling what it was like to go blind?

How she stood in a pasture in fog,
the cows graying, then absent,
then no longer existing?

For years she sat with her little dog,
knitting baby blankets for the hospital.

During which time
all of her friends died, said Mom.

Mom's Playthings

In Mom's window, sheep grazed
on distant, old-fashioned hills

where now great flocks of condos
have come to roost.

Angels with watering cans
made the rain,

but no one remembers what doll
or animal drowsed in her bed with her.

Her playthings sleep
somewhere in tissue now,
no one knows where.

Somewhere no longer in existence.

The Lullabies of Elsewhere

She was always elsewhere.

That's what Mom wants
carved on her stone.

When did she first realize
there *was* an Elsewhere,
and that she was in it?

What baby songs did she
sing from wherever she was
down to me in my crib?

The lullabies of Elsewhere.

On birthdays
she filled little flowerpots
with chocolate ice cream

and a real zinnia,
chocolate jimmies for dirt.

I tasted the cold chocolate,
I opened the gifts.

If they were real, I was real.
I was in the Elsewhere, too.

No Blue Allowed

No blue allowed on the tree.

The kids would hide tiny objects
deep inside the branches—

gems of blue Life Savers here and there,
camouflaged, glued to a bird's wing.

When Mom saw blue her eyes
would stop on it overlong,

but she'd say nothing.

Blue hit a cold note
among the fire-like reds and golds,
the Christmas golds and greens.

Bermuda Sand

Mom has a beau at Stone Ridge

whose wife no longer loves him.

When the wife is ill, the two of them
dine together in plain sight
and no one knows.

Eighty-five and eighty-eight, in love!

Her apartment's new paint color
is Bermuda Sand, *a neutral
with character,* as Mom puts it.

Tonight she's cooking red snapper for one
with green beans and baby potatoes,
good colors on one of Grandma's plates.

Melancholy, such beauty seen alone.

After her bath and her lotions,
she'll swipe clean the clouded mirror,
dip a tiny brush in its bottle.

She's whitening the teeth in her skull.

Mom Looking Skinny

Bermuda, 1958

The family's sitting on the pink bungalow steps,
the couple and the two daughters, six and eight.

A stranger walking by took the shot:
four late-afternoon shadows.

Mom's only jewelry is her collarbone.

She hugs her long shins,
kneecaps distinct, shanks and shins
and sandaled feet, the foot bones

clusters of twigs and nacreous shells.
Underlying the beautiful wife-skin

is the young skeleton laid bare.

The day's adventure was a trip
to the Horses' Graveyard.

You have to walk far from the village,
far from the pink-white tourist beaches.

The sea has eaten out a narrow cove,
coral pocked and piled up in porous chunks,
so sharp that a mere brush across it

raises pin-lines of blood which
rinse away and re-form.

All the whole skulls have been taken,

but teeth are plentiful, and vertebrae.
Racks of bleached ribs emerge,
picked clean by turkey vultures and crabs,

blasted by sand. They bury the horses,
then let the storms take them.

Dismantling the bodies is the waves' work.

The children gather teeth. They see
the shock of a horse only half-consumed

by carrion eaters and the sea, snagged on rocks.

Meat, with bones emerging and the skull
already gone—somewhere an empty head—

and the tail washing back and forth in the shallows.

Mom's Red Convertible

Mom has three walkers.
Her favorite, her red convertible,
wobbles, and is being repaired.

The new one is not really red.
More like magenta. All wrong.
She's sending it back.

Then there's the drugstore model,
aluminum, folding, black, light—
the one that goes in the car.

The red convertible is the exact red
of her first bicycle,
which she wishes she still had.

Of all the walkers,
it's the only *elegant* one.
It has good bones, says Mom.

I picture the red convertible
back in its early days,
speedy and sleek.

I picture the red convertible
parked in a dark workshop,
waiting for someone to come fix it.

Babylon at Stonehenge

Mom calls Stone Ridge, her retirement community,
Stone*henge.* And Avalon, the skilled-nursing wing,

she calls *Babylon,* because to her it seems
the outer limits of what one should have to bear.

She's thinking of the ancient city, briefly holy
and briefly the empire's capital, before it was

destroyed and rebuilt repeatedly over centuries.

‡

Mom says she has a new love interest.
Wonderful! What's his name?

After a long pause she says, *Ask me later.*

‡

The Lindbergh baby ruined Mom's childhood.

Because of the scare, parents became hypervigilant,
keeping their children close to them at all times.

No more walking to school alone.

But Mom could go anywhere—
ride her bike to the matinee in town,

hide in the attic, and no one would worry
because her parents did not keep her close.

The Lindbergh baby cast a permanent
harsh light on Florence and Rodney.

‡

In Babylon, the nurses change shifts.
Who can keep track of them?

It's always a stranger who bathes her.

She's almost a ghost, a see-through
idea of herself, catching feathers
dropped from a very distant bird.

Her childhood was a snowfall of down,

and now there's hardly
a feather in the house.

‡

Mom is unhappy at Stonehenge.
It's too isolated.

But Mom, you moved here because
you were lonely in Rhode Island.

It was too remote. Besides,
you have friends here.

Nonsense. I have way
more friends in Rhode Island.

But you don't seem to be in touch
with them anymore.

That's because they're all dead.

The Floatisphere

Mom has had a seizure.
Four seizures, and a fall.

She is relieved to find herself
not in the hospital

but back in her own bed after all.

I'm in the Floatisphere, she says,
where everything is just as it was.

I'm glad she can still talk to me
from so far away, in the Floatisphere,

where Death marries whatever it loves.

Movies of Mountains

What a find—a box of stuttering,
skinny reels and Dad's projector.

When he's shooting, the camera strays
from kid in stroller to mountains beyond,

then stays on the mountains,
panning up the north flank of Giant

then down the slides left
by the avalanche, 1963.

That view, in every weather.
Rain-grayed. Stark with ice.

The alpenglow, shot from the back porch
over years through slowly thickening pines.

Dad bought the house the year
they married, without consulting her.

There's the mountain again,
always there behind the house—

grayscale in moonlight,
a great, hulking ghost in snow.

Handwriting's Ancestors

When I took over Dad's finances
I read his check register's

minuscule marginal notes
(many question marks, lists of groceries).

He was living on *the soup that eats like a meal*.
We had to drive him home when his

key wouldn't fit in the radio.
No one could stop

the slow truck of brain damage.
His last letters canted, diminutive

script written as if uphill, petering out
or running off the edge of the page.

Sometimes a tautness enters my hand,
so that my writing becomes slightly

more angular, smaller, with
"shrunken" and "crabbed" in its near future.

Dad's handwriting enters mine
as frost takes the ground.

The Words of His Dementia

I found a letter Dad wrote to Mom
decades after their divorce,

lines of tiny words slanting suddenly
up as they neared the edge of the paper

hitting the brakes just a little late.

I'll try a letter longhand to see how far I can get.

I simply can't make the typewriter
do what I want one to do.

To hell with all machines.
Let's go it the old-fashioned way.

Ermine Tails

In the end, having spurned her walker,
using it mainly to transport
her dinner and glass of wine,

Mom broke her hip furniture-walking,

astonished to learn she did not
invent the technique.

Drugs kept her *comfortable*—

the three daughters thought that
a strange choice of words.

She was half with us, half peering ahead
at whatever it was she could see.

She left behind strange ménages:
towels with first-marriage monograms,
tax returns, scorched pot holders,

Great Gran's lost ring among the forks.

Dad's few remaining things disintegrated
back into the family years ago,

so these boxes contain
the last of the evidence, last clues.

Mom saved stationery three addresses old.

She saved my plastic horses, neighing
and stamping in their shoebox barn.

Cary tried on the dress with ermine tails.
Who wore it, and on what occasion?

Macabre, the little white tails whispering
to one another across her breast.

Here's a pair of tiny deerskin shoes,
a sweater, half-knitted, in a plastic bag.

Now that I'm no longer a daughter,
I don't know what to wear.

Animals, Not Initials

The crematorium sent Mom's ashes
via UPS, which left them on the porch
with the mail. In the box,

a card taped to a plastic urn bore
her name in schoolgirl calligraphy.

A name on a stone. How soon
no one remembers the person.

Watering her flowers, Mom left
sepia footprints on the slates.

Painters of caves left handprints
the colors of charcoal, pulverized rock.

Also legs and horns, outlines of lives—

antelope, bison, and bear.
Come to me, crude animals.

Tell me where you are now.

The M Sound

First baby-sound,
Ma, Mom, Mummy,

the lips gathering and then releasing
their desire for milk,

like a kiss.

And now *marble, melancholy,
memento.*

It's the sound the mouth makes
the first time it opens
and the last.

Her Ashes

I touched them, her ashes,

when we gathered by the Atlantic's
cold green-gray concussions

to free her, handful by handful,
from the form she had taken in the world.

She was silky and gritty and purified.

I had to rinse her ghost from my hands.

Roadkill

You, Reader, as I Imagine You

Why is it awkward to acknowledge
each other's presence here?

Who says we can't meet in public,
can't stop and sit together on a bench
and watch the dogs go by?

As a child, I looked for you
in books and sometimes sensed
you (reading what I was reading).

Even as a child I knew you would
someday come to this place to meet me.

Cages for Unknown Animals

That's what I build, trapping only
shadows of their mystery, in traps I abandon
since shadows also escape them.

I study the places where darkness collects—
always cageless, always camouflaged—
to see what goes there to drink.

Poems should be made of nothing
but truth and mystery, but either

truth or mystery usually escapes.

Nothing

My teacher asked me if I could accept
practice without realization.

It's a very direct question,
but I had no answer.

I thought of writing on water,
writing on wind,
writing with white on white.

He asked me what was stopping me
from realizing the true nature of my self.

I said, Nothing. He said,
Uh-oh, better be careful!

Roadkill

I want to see things as they are
without me. Why, I don't know.

As a kid I always looked
at roadkill close up, and poked
a stick into it. I want to look at death

with eyes like my own baby eyes,
not yet blinded by knowledge.

I told this to my friend the monk,
and he said, *Want, want, want.*

Invisible Fence

Every moment's a splitting twig,
a wind that blows the smoke
west then blows it east.

A thousand silver minnows of distraction!
And sleep, my Lethe and opium.

Once in a while I catch myself awake.
That breaks the spell,

though a few last splinters of fire
still smoke in the sky, the me,
the open space, the nowhere.

Spaciousness

I saw it for a second, spaciousness—
It wasn't made of air, to my surprise.

Well, *saw* is misleading. I mean
I *perceived* it as the distance

between the self and the reappearance
of its self-regard, vast or minuscule.

If I could diagram it like a machine
in the exploded view—

but of course I can't. And it wasn't
like anything, unless it was like snow,

the way it falls both disturbed
and undisturbed by our lives.

Zazen

Sometimes during zazen
I break a twig on the path
so I can find my way back,

then realize I'll never
pass this way again.

Strange practice, to sit motionless

watching birds of mind
flit among imaginary clouds.

Once in a while, I catch myself
undistracted even by myself.

It's hard to explain
in such featherweight
words as these.

Never

The clouds' disintegrating script
spells out the word *squander*.

Tree shadows lie down in the field.
Clipped to a grass blade's underside,

a crisp, green grasshopper
weighs down the tip,

swaying between birth and death.
I'll think of him as we clink

glasses with the guests,
eating olives as the sun goes down.

The Second Arrow

Someone once asked Shunryu Suzuki Rōshi
why there's so much suffering in the world.

He said, *No reason.*

The Buddha said that suffering
is the first arrow—

injury, injustice, old age, illness, and death.
But it's the second he said to beware.

It might be tiny or even invisible,
with one of the three poisons

glistening at its tip—

anger, delusion, greed.
Their tiny barbs fasten like ticks.

Flags in their three colors
snap above the empires and encampments,

the towers of the rulers, high floors aglow,

and the blanket-and-cardboard towns,
the nests of the fallen in doorways
and under trees

where the air is gray with suffering
but the flags are bright.

I'm building a bonfire of second arrows
to ignite on the occasion of my awakening.

Meanwhile, I come here to swing on long chains
and hear their singsong:

greed-y, greed-y, and the sprinklers:
pissed off, pissed off, pissed off.

The dogs are tearing the white stuffing
out of a toy in Nirvana, right at my feet.

I still don't know what dogs know.

Silence vs. Music

At some point I stopped listening
to music and tuned instead
to the sound behind it,

which is not silence, but space
devoid of anything composed
for human listening.

Wind roughing up the uncut field.
Trucks coughing on the road.

Sometimes I hear voices in the brook,
children mostly, but not their

million useless words. They're just
calling out the sounds the world makes

whether there's a listener or not.

Labradorite

If the sun is out you can see
the gray-green iridescence

embedded in the underwater stones,

a sudden peacock gleam
that hides in the air.

This stone calls forth lost memories,
says my book. It's feldspar—

the cold fire of aurora borealis
crushed by the glacier into sparks.

Sickness and Medicine

Old Nan's hindquarters crunch
when she walks. Sometimes
she carries her left foreleg.

When I bend down to give her
cream cheese with a pill inside,
she licks my own arthritic hand.

The tractor blurts out diesel noise,
blades sparking on hidden stones,
then a wounded silence.

In the just-cut field, a fox
watches each bite of dinner
reveal itself.

Path of Red Leaves

I stop on a footbridge in the old woods,
and look down into the turbulent
gleam of a waterfall's

disappearance into the next pool,
and the gleam of its never leaving.

I've been strolling on a path of red leaves

waiting for a kenshō or a trophy,
for someone to call my name.

Instead, the brook's cold, secret sparks
ask me if I'm immortal, too.

Early Snow

The first snow brings down
a weak branch: dull crack, soft explosion.

Why so many acorns this year?
Is a bad winter coming?

Snow brightens the pond
for not even a second.

What cold dream of beauty
melts in the springlike afternoon?

In their dazzling white slips,
roof and branch are sisters.

Who dreams? Who listens
to the fire come alive in the grate?

Days of Not-Knowing

In my twenties I squandered afternoons
driving somewhere new just for the hell of it,

Amish Kalona or German Amana
or places with names like
Coon Rapids and Beebeetown,

driving or riding in the back of a pickup
to somebody's farmhouse for a party.

Skinny-dipping in Jack's pond.

Some of us naked in public for the first time.

Then all the young poets late in the bars.
Those days of not-knowing I did not know.

I Keep Scaring Myself

The distant fields lie fallow,
no longer even grazed.

Someday I'll be a plow blade
of pelvis, a few long bones.

I keep scaring myself,
but not about the body.

It's about the veils, which feel,
if I raise my arms, like wings—

feathers of white sky, word-shreds
in which I conceal myself.

Part of me wants to go live
with the woman in a nursing home

whose suitor brings her the same
gold earrings every day in a box
with fresh paper and ribbon.

Each time I see them is the first time.

Falling Leaves

In the skylight, no sky.

Just a flurry of papery fire colors
on their way to earth.

My mind tries to snare
this beauty, chasing
its memorial shadows.

Falling leaf!
Stop for a second
so I can write on you.

Nan's Stick

Barely forty degrees,
windy and clear. Nothing
could have grown overnight,

not a single seed sprouted,

but the dog and I patrol
the garden anyway, the beds
of frost-ruckled dirt

just opened, just turned,
raspberry and blueberry shoots
vivid with early greens,

little tomato plants
looking green and stalwart
under plastic domes.

I poke a radish seed
under, and pulverize a ball
of soil to fill my print.

Nan carries her stick.

Fox Bones

To write a poem is to study oneself.
To strip away all but the sinews,
and then the sinews.

A jawbone stuck out of the dirt—
young fox with still-perfect teeth.
I keep it on my desk.

Everything is made of mystery.
And then it all disappears.

Two Dogs Passing Through the Yard

One's a male Aussie mix,
either young or small, the other
a rangy Lab-something, female,
the junior dog, both headed north
through the yard.

Our Border-Aussie
watches from beneath the truck,
paws crossed.

That's it.

Now's Dream

The Park from Above

What scared them? Scores of wild green parrots
fly up shrieking out of the palms,

circle and return, settling their now-invisible wings.

A man has crawled out of the mangroves,
zipping his fly. It's the spot where the dogs
always stop overlong, then look at me as if to say,

Explain this, please. It's the guy who sleeps
on a nearby bench and loiters by the boat launch.

The dogs sniff out a roll of toilet paper in a plastic bag,
hidden behind leaves with his backpack and tarp.

The only other witnesses are two white ibis
nervous on the concrete seawall, swiveling

their slender necks, which look too thin
to swallow anything. They fly when we come near,
up to join the ruckus of small green angels

hidden in the palms or spiraling up into the realm

just above the human one, from which they can see
the silver streams of traffic, small figures walking dogs,

the glass and plastic mysteries delivered by the tide.

The Feeder of Strays

Someone leaves chicken bones in the park

among the nuggets of bark mulch.
A splintery cooked bone can kill a dog.

Mom is dead. Three months now.

Four times a day, beneath the palms,
Rebus and I follow the piss-tags along the paths.

After dark we follow the Feeder of Strays.
Rebus noses out the bones. I confiscate them

and throw them away with the shit.

Bipolar II-ity

Though I'm actually depressive with ADHD,
a doctor once diagnosed me as Bipolar II.

For ten months I lived in
a sequence of places foreign to me.

Actually, the places weren't foreign,
though I was a tourist there.

A sequence of tourists.

Sometimes I was a river that forked,
then forked again, each time asking,

The other river, where did it go?

Being a river was a kind of mental suffering
new to me, not kin to me.

Wrong branch of the tree.

The Duck Boat

Twenty-two floors below us,
at the private marina and public boat launch,

something's always going on.

Four times a day, the Duck Boat
drives down the ramp into Biscayne Bay

carrying its cargo of tourists into the floating world,
bus one minute, boat the next,
bound for the islands of the rich and famous.

The water amplifies even small sounds:
someone unlocking the yacht club gate

for caterers, who wheel their white carts
down the long dock to the boat throwing a party.

Police ticketing Jet Skiers for lacking life jackets.

At dusk a school of paddleboards
returns from the islands,

trailing underwater neon lights.

I imagine this vista fifty years from now,
towers rising straight out of the water,

their top floors lit by fires, where survivors
tie their boats to balcony railings.

In the meantime, four times a day,

the amphibious tourists quack
loudly as the Duck Boat hits the bay.

Buzzyboy

Buzzyboy's right on schedule,

at the public boat launch, gassed up
and in the water by 4:20 every afternoon.

He does tricks for a couple of hours—

tight figure eights so he can hit
his own wake
twice, using the up-kick to flip entirely,

the two of them one circle, him and his
beautiful sleek black seal of a machine.

I watch him with binoculars
from the twenty-second floor.

I can also look directly down
into the yacht club's white precincts,

its sixty white sea-houses
tethered in their slips,

and one wooden cabin cruiser from the 1950s,
dark among the icebergs.

Someone's having a party. Through a porthole
I can see origami-flower hors d'oeuvres,
bright petals to eat.

Watch out, there's a lot of broken glass

by the boat launch. Big weekend out there
on the water, tourists and locals both.

They all leave their shopping carts
in the parking lot for someone to pick up.

But who? Underlings from Big Market,
of course. Cart jockeys. Jobs.

A River in Egypt

Denial is not a river in Egypt
says my T-shirt, once Dad's.

But it is, with its crocodiles and palms,

and all the answers flying this way,
little vanilla egrets low over the water,

over the banked crocodiles snoozing
in the long self-sharpening shadows

which fall also on a table for one, on a balcony
overlooking a fork in my river in Egypt.

I have a perfect view of the place where one river
becomes two, as if a mirror could be divided,

or a wishbone split itself.

Denial splits the mind, making one part
invisible to the other.

The two are strangers when they
sit next to each other on the train

that makes rough music of *Now or never*
now or never now. Never now.

Ghost Dress

On a hanger the pattern tissues
for the new dress stir as I pass:

the still-perfect ghost dress

not yet cut, not worn or worn out,
not given away or sent to Goodwill.

I lay out the indigo silk on the cutting grid.

Mom gave me her whole stash
the year she donated her machine
to the Visiting Nurses.

This is the first piece of it I've cut.

The near-weightless spirits lie down
upon it, and I pin them there.

The scissors come seeking them out.

The Phantoms for Which Clothes Are Designed

Sewing patterns are designed for imaginary
people, based on average measurements
taken in the 1930s by the WPA

and adjusted over the decades by the Industry.

I sew a misses 14, designed for a woman
5'5" to 5'6", 36"/28"/38",

which is to say no one,

so I alter the pattern to fit a phantom of me
instead of a phantom of her.

She doesn't need any more dresses.

Murder and Mayhem in Miami

That's what we call the evening news.

Shootings, of course, dropping or throwing
babies from high windows, animal cruelty,

of course. But also strange crimes and actions
you'd think would be rare but are very common:

Driving a vehicle into a building,
often day care or a church.

Importing exotic wildlife,
anything endangered or rare,

especially snakes that eat live prey.

At the airport a man carried
his pygmy marmoset under his shirt
through the X-ray,

insisting that all the bones
belonged to a single soul.

Sinkholes appear.
Houses disappear.

People steal ATMs
with a truck and a chain.

We're in full-blown end-of-world mind
here in Miami.

The bay licks at the lowest balconies

night after night. Already barnacles
have attached to their undersides.

The Wrong House

Russell and I almost bought
a wrong house. Well, we didn't
almost buy it, but we really did

try it on for size.
Yes, we could live there.

It was a very strange house,
with two front doors and five back doors.

An above-ground pool sat atop
a sort of altar, a stone pedestal,

so you had to climb a ladder to get in.

Maybe because Mom died
and we left our beautiful Miami

all in one year—
one gravestone, one mirage—

we were rash even to consider it.

But it had a view of Japan,
a view of Spain!

Fireworks or Gunfire?

It's just somebody sighting his gun—
deer season opens on Friday.

In the north country, many people hunt.
Bow hunting, crossbow, muzzle-loader,

then long guns, and guns with scopes.

First birds, then bear, bobcat, deer,
and finally, the smaller furbearers. Traps.

In Miami, my first thought
would have been fireworks.

Any occasion, any time of year,
from rooftops, condo balconies, private yards—

people there like to shoot bright unfurling
pink and green chrysanthemums into the sky,

then watch all their petals come apart.

Of course there was gunfire in Miami too,
all the time, mostly handguns

and assault rifles, but always far away—
in a mall, on I-90, in the Gardens, on TV,

though a man in our building was shot,
and another in the park next door.

Love in one case, drugs in the other.

It's strange to think of Miami now,
here in the north woods as tiny pearls of sleet
begin to fill the crisp cups of leaves.

Ancient Questions

Why must I settle for myself
the ancient questions?

No one asked me to.

I look up. These leaves are the embers
of the peak: darker, more intense, finally

devoid of green, which I find more beautiful.

I choose between them. Why?
Are they not a single autumn?

I see that all questions collapse
into one, but what is it?

Why do I still not know its words?

The cold brook of striving talks to me at night.
It says, *Wake up. Stop doing anything else.*

Is that a calling? It's not an invitation.

Now's Dream

My understanding is
that what I call my Self

is asleep, and has dreamed up

these lilacs excited by sudden
thunder-dark, the birds gone still.
A purple trembling.

But how do I know I'm dreaming?

And how did I come to imagine
I might wake up?

That there's something to wake from,
and what that something is?

Lilacs—totem. They smell of grief,

so they must be my lilacs.
I must have dreamed them up,

stowed them away in me

so I could stand near them now,
this very afternoon, down near the pond
before it pocks with rain.

Now it's in smithereens.

What's Wrong with Me

The end of the world
is not what's wrong with me.

Old age, illness, and death
are not wrong. They just are.

A stone says, *Wake up,*
exactly this is all there is!

Everything says it—

a sick coyote crossing the field,
poisoned, injured, rabid, old,

the rest of the pack anxious,
yipping and howling back and forth
across the valley as dusk comes on.

What's wrong with me is that
I find their music beautiful.

I dwell on it long after it stops,
and in the silence afterward

I write down its words.

Toygers

In a litter of mackerel tabbies,
one kitten had a strange face
with black parentheses, like a tiger's.

Desire sank its claws in a breeder's mind.

She searched the world for cats with the same
genetic mutation,

street cats in India, shelter cats, purebred rejects,

and over twenty years produced
her imaginary animal, the Toyger.

Among other qualities, *Natural "make-up"*
is important: eyes must have black "mascara"
markings and whited spectacles, desirable

for mouth to have black lipstick markings.

Will that be adequate camouflage
in fifty years or a hundred years?

I hope these little tiger-creatures survive.

I hope they go feral, proliferate,
drive the rats from New York, and restore

harmony and order to the universe.

Plain American

The dog and I climb to a high ledge
shagged with juniper,

from which we can see the house and garden
below us diffused in falling snow.

Rebus sniffs out a freshly killed
porcupine, quill-side down.

A fisher will slit the belly
with a single claw, leaving
nothing but a scalp of quills.

A treasure for a kid, that pelt.

But confiscated today—
no good for dogs. Sorry, Rebus.

I'll do something with the quills.
Glue them to a mirror frame.

I want to write poems
in plain American which cats and dogs can read!
as Marianne Moore put it,

though I doubt that cats and dogs
will ever read them.

Rebus says, *Let's get going.*

He knows I've got the porcupine
in my pack, in a plastic ziplock.

Things as It Is

Last night my hand began writing
in the hand of some future me,
as if a branch in wind had scribbled

on freshly fallen snow.
In the dark, coyotes called

back and forth in the bird-silence.

I put down the pen and went outside,
stood listening to wind in snow's translation.

Wild dogs, teach me
a few of your words before I die.

Kenshō of Ash

Smoke, snow, ash, rain, wind—

five elements of winter here
in the north country just before spring,

people still burning wood.

A pair of downy woodpeckers
raids the suet, nesting nearby,

the male sparrow-size,
black-and-white,

slash of red
on the black crown—

he might be the last bird I ever see.

I might go blind, or die,
or all birds go suddenly extinct.

Consciousness *will* end.
It could happen at any time.

What's this? Not snow but ash,
tiny cold petals in the air—

a neighbor burning brush.

I put down the saw
to watch the brief flurry.

I'm building a birdhouse
in case any birds survive.

Winter Crows

A few overwinter, the breeding pairs.
I like their ruckus in the early spring—

stealing bristles right off
the broom still frozen on the deck

and the dog hair I put out for them
when I clip him. Rebus has wool—

brown curls. The crows carry off
every strand of it, up to the sky

where they weave and knot it
with great economy into their

big, minimalist baskets of twig
and grapevine, which they line

with mosses, dog hair, ribbons of birch bark,

and withered iris blades worried from
the thawing shallows of the pond.

I count at least nine nests in the oak,
upheld in the great high branches,

a tilted candelabrum
that goes slowly dark at night.

Fast Stars

I love the way snow first
sharpens the branches,
then gradually, softly, erases them.

No, *I* sharpen and soften and erase them.

I repeatedly forget that I'm god of this place.

I once imagined Nirvana lay just beyond
the smoke and dark of human craziness,

this wilderness of ruins,

as if there were a border somewhere
not far off that I would someday cross

when it was time,
and that there would be time.

The fast stars rising from the fires
I kindle and tend
are all my own creation,

as is this graffiti, which lasts
no longer than perfume.

The temperature's dropping fast,
bound for below zero.

Again I've made it too cold
for the animals tonight,

too cold for myself.

I'll camp here in the hinterland
just outside Nirvana.

The deer will dig snow beds;
the otters will not fish.

Notes

Book epigraph—The quote is from *Zen Is Right Here: Teaching Stories and Anecdotes of Shunryu Suzuki,* edited by David Chadwick (Shambhala, 2001). The *Sandōkai,* sometimes translated as the Identity of Relative and Absolute, is an eighth-century poem written by Shih-t'ou Hsi-ch'ien (Sekitō Kisen in Japanese). It is a fundamental text of the Sōto school.

"Maverick"—The theme song for the TV series *Maverick* (1957-1962) was written by David Buttolph (music) and Paul Francis Webster (lyrics). The poem plays with lines from the song.

"The Ghost of Tom"—Folk song whose date, author, and composer are unknown:

Have you seen the ghost of Tom?
Long white bones with the rest all gone.
Oh oh oh oh oh oh oh,
Wouldn't it be chilly with no skin on?

"Tender Shepherd" ("The Ghost of Tom")—A song written for the musical *Peter Pan,* 1954, music by Moose Charlap and Jule Styne and lyrics by Carolyn Leigh, Betty Comden, and Adolph Green.

"Sad Song"—The last line and a half are from Bob Dylan's "Girl from the North Country."

"The Uphill River"—

This is the thing—if you see how things are, "things-as-it-is" as Suzuki Rōshi used to say, you see that they arise and they pass away. The trick is to live in harmony with the way things actually are. Our suffering comes from wanting things to be different than they are. You know, like trying to push the river uphill.

—Zenkei Blanche Hartman, "A Natural Action" (2000)

"Handwriting's Ancestors"—*The soup that eats like a meal* is a 1985 slogan for the Campbell Soup Company's Chunky Soups.

"Zazen"—*Zazen* is Zen seated meditation.

"The Second Arrow"—The Shunryu Suzuki story is recounted in *Zen Is Right Here,* ed. Chadwick.

Kenshō ("Path of Red Leaves," "Kenshō of Ash")—In Zen Buddhism, kenshō is a sudden, brief glimpse into the true nature of being. It is not enlightenment, but rather a door to greater realization.

"Toygers"—The lines in italic are taken from the International Cat Association (TICA)'s 2003 Breed Standards for the Toyger.

"Plain American"—The quoted line is from Marianne Moore's "England," in *The Poems of Marianne Moore,* edited by Grace Schulman (Penguin, 2005).

‡

Personals:

"The Hill Towns of Connecticut" and "Soft Leather Reins" are for Sarah Nettleton, "The Wrong House" for Terry McCormack DeBrule, and "Kenshō of Ash" for Tom Smith. Geoffrey Shugen Arnold Rōshi: no words.

About the Author

Chase Twichell has published seven previous books of poetry, most recently *Horses Where the Answers Should Have Been: New and Selected Poems* (Copper Canyon, 2010), which won both the Kingsley Tufts Poetry Award from Claremont Graduate University and the Balcones Poetry Prize from Austin Community College. Her work has received fellowships and awards from the National Endowment for the Arts, the John Simon Guggenheim Memorial Foundation, the American Academy of Arts and Letters, and the Poetry Society of America. After teaching for many years (Hampshire College, the University of Alabama, and Princeton University), she quit academia to start Ausable Press, a not-for-profit publisher of poetry that was acquired by Copper Canyon in 2009. Since 1996 she has been a student in the Mountains and Rivers Order at Zen Mountain Monastery. She lives in upstate New York with her husband, the novelist Russell Banks.

Poetry is vital to language and living. Since 1972, Copper Canyon Press has published extraordinary poetry from around the world to engage the imaginations and intellects of readers, writers, booksellers, librarians, teachers, students, and donors.

WE ARE GRATEFUL FOR THE MAJOR SUPPORT PROVIDED BY:

THE PAUL G. ALLEN
FAMILY FOUNDATION

Anonymous

Jill Baker and Jeffrey Bishop

Anne and Geoff Barker

Donna and Matt Bellew

John Branch

Diana Broze

Sarah and Tim Cavanaugh

Beatrice R. and Joseph A. Coleman Foundation

Laurie and Oskar Eustis

Mimi Gardner Gates

Linda Gerrard and Walter Parsons

Nancy Gifford

Gull Industries Inc.
on behalf of Ruth and William True

The Trust of Warren A. Gummow

Phil Kovacevich and Eric Wechsler

Lakeside Industries Inc.
on behalf of Jeanne Marie Lee

TO LEARN MORE ABOUT UNDERWRITING
COPPER CANYON PRESS TITLES,
PLEASE CALL 360-385-4925 EXT. 103

WE ARE GRATEFUL FOR THE MAJOR SUPPORT PROVIDED BY:

Maureen Lee and Mark Busto
Rhoady Lee and Alan Gartenhaus
Ellie Mathews and Carl Youngmann as The North Press
Anne O'Donnell and John Phillips
Petunia Charitable Fund and adviser Elizabeth Hebert
Gay Phinney
Suzie Rapp and Mark Hamilton
Emily and Dan Raymond
Jill and Bill Ruckelshaus
Kim and Jeff Seely
Richard Swank
University Research Council of DePaul University
Vincentian Endowment Foundation
Dan Waggoner
Barbara and Charles Wright
Caleb Young and Keep It Cinematic
The dedicated interns and faithful volunteers
of Copper Canyon Press

The Chinese character for poetry is made up of two parts: "word" and "temple." It also serves as pressmark for Copper Canyon Press.

This book is set in Farnham, designed by Christian Schwartz. Book design by VJB/Scribe. Printed on archival-quality paper.